AF228523

Handling
Autism

by Racquel Foran

Content Consultant

Cassandra Sanchez, PsyD
Postdoctoral Psychology Fellow
University of Southern California
University Center for Excellence in
Developmental Disabilities

Handling
Health Challenges

Essential Library
An Imprint of Abdo Publishing
abdobooks.com

abdobooks.com

Published by Abdo Publishing, a division of ABDO, PO Box 398166, Minneapolis, Minnesota 55439. Copyright © 2022 by Abdo Consulting Group, Inc. International copyrights reserved in all countries. No part of this book may be reproduced in any form without written permission from the publisher. Essential Library™ is a trademark and logo of Abdo Publishing.

Printed in China.
052021
092021

Cover Photo: iStockphoto
Interior Photos: iStockphoto, 4, 9, 12, 28, 31, 35, 38, 40, 64, 71, 75; FatCamera/iStockphoto, 16, 48, 68; Haraz N. Ghanbari/AP Images, 18; Africa Studio/Shutterstock Images, 23; Photographee.eu/Shutterstock Images, 43; May Tse/South China Morning Post/Getty Images, 47; Andrey Popov/iStockphoto, 50; NLM/Science Source, 53; Jodi Cobb/National Geographic Image Collection/Alamy, 57; Sebastian Kaulitzki/Science Source, 60; SDI Productions/iStockphoto, 77; Loic Venance/AFP/Getty Images, 78; Kathryn Scott/Denver Post/Getty Images, 83; Steven Wright/Shutterstock Images, 87; Pu Ying Huang/AP Images, 91; Rich Graessle/Icon Sportswire/AP Images, 92; Nora Tam/South China Morning Post/Getty Images, 97

Editor: Alyssa Krekelberg
Series Designer: Megan Ellis

Library of Congress Control Number: 2020948042

Publisher's Cataloging-in-Publication Data

Names: Foran, Racquel, author.
Title: Handling autism / by Racquel Foran
Description: Minneapolis, Minnesota : Abdo Publishing, 2022 | Series: Handling health challenges | Includes online resources and index.
Identifiers: ISBN 9781532194948 (lib. bdg.) | ISBN 9781098215255 (ebook)
Subjects: LCSH: Autism--Juvenile literature. | Autism spectrum disorders--Juvenile literature. | Autistic people--Juvenile literature. | Autism--Diagnosis--Juvenile literature. | Autism in children--Treatment--Juvenile literature. | Health--Juvenile literature.
Classification: DDC 616.8982--dc23

Contents

Chapter
One

Living with Autism

Matthew's day begins exactly how he likes it, with his mom opening his bedroom door at 8:15 and saying, "Rise and shine, Matthew! It's another new day." To this, Matthew always responds, "Which new day?" and then his mom tells him what day it is. Once Matthew knows what day it is, he knows what he must prepare for. Today is Monday.

After he wakes, Matthew goes to the kitchen, where his mom has a bowl of granola with sliced bananas waiting for him. From eating he goes directly to the bathroom, where he brushes his teeth and washes his face and hands—always in that order. He then goes to his bedroom, where his mom has laid out his clothes. On Mondays he wears a blue shirt. He is always ready and waiting exactly five minutes

Having autism affects the daily life of the individual and those close to him or her.

before 9:00 a.m. for his transportation to arrive. He does not like it when the van is late.

It is important to Matthew that he start his day this way. He also feels the need to stick just as strictly to the rest of his routines and schedule. Matthew has autism, and like many people on the autism spectrum, he finds comfort in routines. Although it's hard for Matthew to let people know what he likes, it's clear that he feels uncomfortable when his routines are disrupted. If everything goes as expected, Matthew proceeds with little emotion or expression, completing each task in an orderly and precise way. But when a routine is broken, Matthew quickly becomes agitated. His parents call these instances meltdowns or sensory overloads.

What Is Neurodiversity?

Originally coined by Australian sociologist Judy Singer in 1998, the term *neurodiversity* refers to the range of brain function people show. This includes social and communication skills, learning ability, and mood. Neurodiversity refers to all brains being different. Therefore, disorders such as autism do not make individuals flawed, just different from typical. Singer, who has autism herself, championed the term because she did not view autism as a disability. Removing the stigma of disability from the equation helps people with autism focus on their strengths instead of their perceived deficits.

Matthew keeps busy with his weekly routine. In addition to attending high school for four hours each weekday, he also takes part in an after-school program that teaches life skills to teens with special needs. But that is not all that keeps him occupied. Matthew has academic tutoring one hour each Monday, soccer practice on Tuesday and Saturday, and basketball on Sunday. On Friday nights he goes to a social club where he gets to hang out with his friends. In his spare time, Matthew is almost always playing games on his computer.

Daily Differences

In many ways Matthew's life is a lot like any other 17-year-old's, but in other ways it is not. For example,

Matthew does not have a job because he struggles with managing his temper. He does not like to make mistakes and sometimes gets easily frustrated. Because he is six feet, two inches (1.9 m) tall and weighs more than 200 pounds (91 kg), his anger may seem scary to other people. Anger management is one of the things that he works on at his life skills program. But until he learns to control his temper, he cannot work. It is a goal he is working hard to achieve.

Another way Matthew's life differs from those of other young people his age is that he spends a lot of time with his parents. Unlike most parents, their responsibilities did not ease as Matthew got older, and they are kept busy with his routine. Friday night social club includes his parents and his friends' parents sitting at an adjoining table at the restaurant. Going to the movies means going with his mom, dad, or older sister. He usually takes trips to the mall with his mom. It's helpful for Matthew to have a trusted adult with him to make sure he's safe. His mom, dad, or sister can remind him to take a break and use coping strategies if he gets overwhelmed. Matthew will likely never live independently. This is something that is a constant source of worry for his parents.

Structure and predictability can make people with autism feel secure and safe. Disruptions to routine can make them feel overwhelmed.

Matthew's parents are relatively young and healthy, and they can attend to his needs. But as they get older or if they face any health challenges themselves, this will change. They live with the fear that no one else will understand and love Matthew as much as they do. In addition to planning and managing his day-to-day needs and activities, they also must plan far into the future. Care and financial needs must be considered beyond their lifetimes. Matthew is lucky because he has an older sister who will be there for him while she is able. But this affects her future too. For example, she plans to never move away from her hometown. That way, she will always be close to Matthew.

Matthew's friends are different too, because autism affects each of them in its own way. For example, his best friend, Kyle, does not like loud noises, flashing lights, or big crowds, so he is not part of the Friday night social club and he does not play on any of Matthew's sports teams. Kyle also rarely speaks. He can, but doing so makes him anxious so he prefers not to. Matthew and Kyle always meet at one of their houses, where they usually play video games together in comfortable silence.

Matthew's friend Spencer is completely different from

Kyle. Spencer talks a lot and can be very loud. He does not fully understand social cues. Sometimes Spencer doesn't know when to stop talking or how people feel when he talks loudly. Spencer gets very excited to share his ideas, and it can be hard for him to do it in a way that feels comfortable for his friends. Spencer also has a part-time job at a grocery store where he packs bags and collects shopping carts.

Spencer has an older brother, John, who also has autism. Like Spencer, John is high functioning. He is studying computer science at college and hopes to get a job with a well-known technology company when he completes his degree. If John is not attending class, he is probably studying. Aside from his near-obsessive studying, the only obvious signs that John is on the autism spectrum are that he keeps his room in precise order, he gets overly agitated when someone disrupts his studying, and he uses overly formal language in casual situations.

Matthew's day ends much like it began. He starts getting ready to go to bed within an hour after eating dinner. His mom leaves out his pajamas in the bathroom. He brushes his teeth and takes a shower. When he is done in the bathroom, he goes to his room, where his mom waits. "What time is it, Mom?" he asks every night as he enters his room. His mom

Autism can make social interactions and eye contact difficult.

responds, "Why, it's bedtime, Matthew." Matthew smiles at his mom and climbs into his bed. His mom tucks the covers in around him and kisses his forehead. Both are ready to follow the same routine again the next day.

What Is Autism?

Although Matthew and his friends are fictional characters, their daily lives reflect the realities of some people who live with autism spectrum disorder (ASD). The *Diagnostic and Statistical*

Restrictive Repetitive Behaviors

RRBs involve five areas. One is repetitive movement with objects, such as repeatedly rolling toy trucks back and forth. Another is compulsive body movements such as rocking, tapping, or swaying the head. RRBs can also include limited, singular, or obsessive interests; sensory sensitivities to things such as bright lights, sudden or loud noises, or large crowds; and insistence on routines or rituals.

RRBs are considered one of the core characteristics of ASD. However, although they are prevalent in people with ASD, they are not exclusive to ASD. It is believed the RRBs people exhibit are ways of soothing themselves when experiencing sensory overload.

Manual of Mental Disorders, Fifth Edition (DSM-5) defines ASD as a developmental disorder. It is characterized by issues with social communication and interactions, as well as restrictive repetitive behaviors (RRBs). Some people may struggle with nonverbal skills. Others may show RRBs such as hand flapping or rocking. However, there is no one-size-fits-all look for autism. Its impact varies greatly

"If you have met one person with autism, you've met one person with autism."[2]

—Dr. Stephen Shore, autism advocate who is on the spectrum, on how unique the disorder is to each person

between individuals. Most children with autism start showing signs of this disorder between the ages of 12 and 18 months.

The term *autism* was first used in the United States in the 1940s by Dr. Leo Kanner. Kanner described children he had observed who showed little interest in others and were quite content to be alone with themselves. Despite extensive studies and many theories, the cause of autism is not known. There is also no known cure. In the last few decades there has been a significant increase in the number of people diagnosed with autism in the United States, jumping from one in 150 children in 2000 to one in 54 in 2016.[3] Medical experts are not sure why there has been a large increase, but most believe it is due to testing increases as well as testing children at younger ages. In other words, the prevalence has not necessarily increased, but rather experts are getting better at diagnosing ASD.

Although there are still many unanswered questions about ASD, strides have been made in improving the lives of those who live with autism. For instance, early testing and diagnoses are increasing. There are also more support groups and resources available for family members and people with autism.

Childhood Disintegrative Disorder

Childhood disintegrative disorder (CDD) was first noted in 1908 by Austrian teacher Theodor Heller. He observed children who were developing social and communication skills as expected suddenly regress into what are now recognized as autism symptoms in toddlers. CDD differentiates itself from autism with its often late and sudden onset. Children who appear to be developing typically up to age ten suddenly lose speech and have other social and communication challenges seen in ASD. The regression is rapid, taking anywhere from months to days. Because of its similarities to autism and equally mysterious cause, CDD is no longer a stand-alone diagnosis in the *DSM-5* but rather falls within the definition of ASD. However, because it presents with unique characteristics, some clinicians still use the term to describe certain cases of autism.

Chapter
Two

Symptoms and Diagnosis

Physicians and parents can use different assessment tools to see whether a child might have autism. One assessment is called the Modified Checklist for Autism in Toddlers, Revised (M-CHAT-R). This checklist evaluates children ages 16 to 30 months for autism. It is a series of 20 questions doctors can ask parents to determine whether further assessment is necessary.

There are specific milestones and behaviors neurotypical babies should achieve by certain ages that the M-CHAT-R screens for. Not reaching some of these milestones is considered an early diagnostic indicator of ASD. One sign that a child may have ASD is that she does not respond to her name by the time she's one year old. Another is if a 14-month-old does not point at things that she is interested in.

If a medical professional says a child who is age two or older has autism, the diagnosis is usually accurate.

US attorney general Eric Holder spoke at the American Academy of Pediatrics in 2009. This organization is dedicated to giving young people the best health possible.

Other indicators of ASD in young children include showing no interest in pretend play; doing repetitive actions such as spinning, rocking, or flapping arms; and getting unusually upset by a change in routine or environment. Missing these milestones or displaying these behaviors would warrant a discussion with a child's health-care provider about further assessment.

Age of Diagnosis

The American Academy of Pediatrics recommends that all children are screened for ASD between the ages of 18 and 24 months. However, only half of

primary care doctors are
doing ASD screenings.[1]
A 2016 study said that
most parents reported
developmental concerns to
the doctor when the child
was just over two years old,
but a diagnosis was not
usually made until past the
age of four.

Early screening and
diagnosis are important.
The earlier a child is
diagnosed, the earlier he or she can get therapy or
intervention. Some interventions may focus on
improving a child's communication or behaviors.
Studies have shown the later the diagnosis, the less
likely children are to receive these treatments. That's
because a late diagnosis might restrict access to
age-specific government support. Additionally, these
children are more likely to be put on medication.
This may be because of a misdiagnosis of another
condition, leading parents to treat and medicate
the incorrect condition. Other research has shown
that the longer the lag between when parents first
express their concerns and a diagnosis, the more

likely the parents are to try alternative interventions and therapies, such as restrictive diets, which can be controversial.

Traits and Symptoms in Older Children

Despite increased awareness that babies can display early signs of ASD, the disorder is still often not diagnosed until children are older. Symptoms can be mild and therefore get missed. Some people live with high-functioning autism. In cases like this, a child's ability to verbally communicate, sometimes with advanced or very formal vocabulary, causes a diagnosis to be overlooked. In the past, some people with high-functioning autism were said to have Asperger's syndrome. However, the *DSM-5* has put this syndrome under the umbrella of ASD. Asperger's syndrome is no longer its own diagnosis.

As children get older and experience more social situations, the boundaries of their limitations are met. Traits of autism that were previously overlooked now become more apparent. Even those with advanced vocabulary and intellect start to display more obvious symptoms of autism.

The symptoms are called the triad of impairments. This triad includes social interaction, social communication, and RRBs. Social indicators that a child might have ASD include a lack of close friends, a disinterest in playing with others, and refusing to join in on group activities. Other indicators include a lack of desire for physical comfort or hugs, trouble expressing feelings, and difficulty understanding other people's feelings.

Social communication deficits might include a lack of emotion in a person's voice or an unusual voice, such as a singsong or high-pitched voice. Others with communication deficits might not understand questions or might respond to them in an atypical

The Triad of Impairments

Lorna Wing was the mother of a daughter with autism. She was also a psychiatrist who became a dedicated autism researcher. In 1964, when assessing a group of children with special needs for research data she was gathering, she and her research partner, Judith Gould, struggled with the diagnostic categories available to them. Some of the children would meet several of the diagnostic criteria for a specific diagnosis or disorder, but not all. This was where the idea for the triad of impairments first developed. Wing and Gould started to characterize impairments based on social interaction, communication, and imagination. They introduced the idea to others in a 1979 research paper. From there, they started referring to autism as a spectrum disorder. As research evolved, the impairment of social imagination, or pretend play, was replaced in the triad by RRBs.

way, or they may not understand the nuances of language and tone of voice—for example, they may miss humor or sarcasm. Nonverbal indicators of ASD can include making facial expressions that do not match the situation; moving in a clumsy or awkward manner; and experiencing sensitivity to lights, sounds, crowds, textures, or smells.

Children with ASD can appear incredibly inflexible in their ways. Rigid routines, extreme attachment to toys or objects, insistence that furniture or objects are always in the same place, singular or narrow interests, and repetitive behaviors are all diagnostic

Repetitive motions are a sign of ASD. For example, a child might constantly spin the wheels on a toy car.

indicators of ASD. Trained professionals might use a tool called the Autism Diagnostic Observation Schedule (ADOS) to screen kids for ASD.

Overlooked and Late Diagnoses

Girls are frequently overlooked for an ASD diagnosis. Part of this is because girls and boys may display signs of autism differently, and physicians are more well-versed in signs that boys exhibit, such as RRBs. Some researchers suggest that girls might want to connect with people more than boys do, and so they are able to mask their autism for a time. Clinical neuropsychologist Dr. Susan F. Epstein says that girls with autism "might not understand what's going on but they'll try to just go along and imitate what they see. And they may get away with it to third grade or fifth grade, but once they get to junior high and high school, it shows as a problem."[3] Girls who are diagnosed with autism later in life are more likely to have developed anxiety, depression, and low self-esteem.

Sometimes a diagnosis of ASD is not made until adulthood. This is most often the case with those who are considered high functioning. Individuals who are not diagnosed as children often sense something is different about themselves as they enter adulthood. For others, they may not be aware of the difference in themselves but those around them have commented on their oddness or peculiar behaviors. There are screening tools for adults who think they might have ASD. The adult Autism-Spectrum Quotient (AQ) questionnaire can help determine whether further assessment should be considered.

ASD Diagnostic Assessment Tests

There are several different testing tools available for assessing and diagnosing ASD. The M-CHAT-R is a screening questionnaire for toddlers ages 16 to 30 months. The questions are answered by parents and focus on the child's behavior. The Childhood Autism Rating Scale (CARS) is a behavior observation assessment for children two years or older that can be used by parents, teachers, or health-care providers. Neither of these are diagnostic tests. But they are useful references when discussing concerns with health-care providers before an ASD diagnosis is made.

The Autism-Spectrum Quotient (AQ) was designed by Cambridge University's Autism Research Centre to measure characteristics of autism in adults. Like the M-CHAT-R and CARS, the AQ is not a diagnostic tool but rather a test to see whether further assessment is called for. The Autism Diagnostic Observation Schedule–Generic is a standardized assessment for professional use to gauge the social interaction, play, imagination, and communication of children and adults who are suspected to be on the spectrum.

Comorbid Diagnoses

People with autism might have additional underlying heath conditions. When a person has two disorders that exist at the same time and often independently from one another, this is known as comorbidity. Having another health condition in addition to autism can affect whether a person is even diagnosed with ASD.

For example, qualities of attention deficit hyperactivity disorder (ADHD) can sometimes mask that a person has autism. ADHD symptoms can include difficulty focusing in school, sitting still, or making eye contact. These are also signs of autism. If a person is diagnosed with ADHD but not autism as well, this can delay his or her path to getting intervention early. Getting a complete diagnosis of all health problems is an important step to ensuring that a person receives proper care.

In some cases, a comorbid condition can intensify characteristics of autism. The Children's Hospital of Philadelphia highlights the difficulties related to autism and comorbidity:

Diagnosis of comorbidities can be challenging because many people with ASD have difficulty recognizing and communicating their symptoms.

Fragile X Syndrome

Fragile X syndrome is a genetic disorder that causes developmental issues such as learning disabilities. This syndrome is highly heritable and has links to ASD. Ninety percent of males that have fragile X syndrome show autistic-like behaviors including hand flapping, sensory sensitivity, and eye contact avoidance, with 30 percent meeting the diagnostic criteria for autism.[6] The most notable symptom of fragile X is intellectual disability with IQs ranging from almost average for mild cases to a low of 40 in severe cases. For comparison, a neurotypical person's IQ ranges between 85 and 115. Physical symptoms of fragile X include long, narrow facial features, prominent ears, and flat feet. It is now standard practice to test for fragile X syndrome in any child presenting with intellectual disability, developmental delay, or ASD.

Physical discomfort might prompt spikes in self-soothing repetitive behaviors as well as irritability, aggression, self-injury, and other challenging behavioral issues. That makes it difficult to tease out whether these behaviors are related to ASD or to physical discomfort caused by a co-occurring condition.[5]

Health conditions that often accompany autism can include epilepsy and seizures, sleep disorders, ADHD, obesity, depression, anxiety, bipolar disorder, and gastrointestinal disorders. Gastrointestinal disorders can include constipation, hemorrhoids, and irritable bowel syndrome.

Chapter
Three

Causes of Autism

There is no known cause for ASD. Researchers have examined biological, behavioral, and cognitive explanations. Biological studies examine the genetic and environmental components and causes of ASD. Behavioral studies focus more on specific symptoms, presentations, and behaviors that are typical of those with autism. Using scientific hypotheses, cognitive studies try to bridge the gap between the two. That is, these studies look at what is happening with the brain and how that manifests itself into autistic behaviors or actions.

Autism is still diagnosed through behaviors. However, researchers have established that there are strong genetic links, and they also believe there are environmental factors at play. Much more research needs to be done to find a cause, but there have been

Scientists continue to study DNA to determine what genes may be linked to autism.

some interesting discoveries to date.

Genetic Research

Most genetic mutations are inherited from parents, but there are rare mutations that can occur spontaneously in an egg or sperm. This would then lead to the child having a mutation neither parent has. Researchers have focused on these rare mutations because they have been found to contribute to 25 to 30 percent of ASD cases.[1]

ASD is one of the most genetically heritable brain conditions. In the 1970s, researchers began to study autism and twins. Studies have reported that when it comes to identical twins, who have the same genes, if one has autism there's an 80 percent chance the other does too.[2] Fraternal twins are the product of two separate eggs being fertilized.

Twin studies can show how much of a role environment and genetics play in a person's development of a disorder or trait.

They only share 50 percent of their genes. If one fraternal twin has autism, there is a 40 percent chance the other does as well.[5] A 2015 analysis of twin studies confirmed this strong genetic connection.

A 2014 research study found that the risk of autism reoccurring in siblings was 10.1 percent as compared to 0.52 percent in the non-ASD sibling group. The research also found that the recurrence risk for second children was higher at 11.5 percent versus third and subsequent children at 7.3 percent.

The increased risk factor also appeared in maternal half-siblings at 6.5 percent for second siblings and 3 percent for third and later children. The risk recurrence for paternal half-siblings was 2.3 percent.[6] In addition, a 2019 research paper reported that genetics were likely responsible for 80 percent of the risk associated with ASD, while environmental causes accounted for only 20 percent.[7]

Despite these clear genetic links, no autism gene has been found. That is, there is no one specific gene that is consistently mutated in every person with autism. However, researchers have come up with a list of 65 genes they think are strongly linked to ASD. There are more than 200 other genes that researchers think might have weaker connections to the condition.[8]

One gene of interest to researchers is SHANK3. SHANK3 mutations are seen in 1 to 2 percent of people with ASD.[9] Another severe developmental disability called Phelan-McDermid syndrome is characterized by a mutation or an absence of a functional copy of the SHANK3 gene. Approximately 75 percent of people with this syndrome also have ASD.[11] SHANK3 is needed to encode the proteins that are necessary for the junctions between neurons to work properly. A mutation of the gene hinders the role of SHANK3. Among other things, this can affect a chemical messenger called glutamate, which is used to establish memory and learning. An imbalance of glutamate has been linked to ASD.

Environmental Research

Genetics may show the degree to which someone is predisposed to ASD, but it does not show what role environmental factors play in its cause. Researchers have found several nongenetic factors that have links to an increased risk of ASD. Advanced parental age is one of the most consistently identified risk factors. Both older fathers and mothers independently increase risk of ASD. One study found that mothers older than 40 and fathers older than 50 had a higher chance of having a child with autism compared with people in their 20s. However, risk factors are not the same as causes of autism, and parents should not blame themselves if they have a child who has autism.

Having a short interval between pregnancies, defined as less than 12 months, is also a reported increased risk factor for ASD. Researchers think the reason for this may be due to nutrient deprivation, stress, or inflammation. However, they do not have a definitive explanation.

Some studies have also shown a child might be at a higher risk for autism if

Experts say that women should wait at least a year and a half between pregnancies. This gives their bodies time to heal.

his or her mother has metabolic conditions, such as diabetes and hypertension. Research has also suggested that having an infection during pregnancy can increase the risk of ASD. One study of more than two million participants showed that maternal bacterial and viral infections during pregnancy increased ASD risk too.

Some medications that cross the placenta and reach the child have also been found to increase the risk of ASD, including drugs used to treat depression, asthma, and epilepsy. These drugs can also transfer to the child through breast milk. Antiepileptic drugs have consistently been found to increase the risk of ASD if used during pregnancy.

Environmental chemicals are another area being researched as a potential cause of ASD. For example, air pollution may have potentially harmful effects on pregnant women. Two California studies published in 2015 specifically noted the third trimester of pregnancy as the most important exposure window to certain pollutants in the air in terms of increased risk of ASD. However, some studies outside the United States have found no correlation between these pollutants and ASD. Still, there is enough growing evidence to suggest that more research into air pollution and ASD may be worth pursuing.

Unanswered Theories

Sometimes research presents more questions than answers. It can be difficult to prove something one way or another. Many theories surrounding autism are still inconclusive and therefore need more investigation.

The body needs folic acid to produce new cells, particularly red blood cells. Folic acid's relationship to ASD is an example of an area of research that is unresolved. Two separate studies reported an approximate 40 percent reduction in the risk of ASD with folic acid supplement use from preconception into early pregnancy.[14] However, a third study found no correlation between folic acid and ASD.

Researchers have looked into several environmental chemicals and their relationships to autism. But this work has been inconclusive. Two studies looked at the prenatal risk level of exposure to chemicals called polychlorinated biphenyls (PCBs). PCBs are toxic, and they can be found in meat, fish, and dairy. Studies have revealed conflicting results on their association with ASD. One study found a

suggestive association with levels of PCBs and ASD, but the other found no association. There were similar results for two studies looking at bisphenol A (BPA), which is a chemical in certain plastics. One found an association with greater autistic symptoms while the other did not.

Vaccines Do Not Cause Autism

Although researchers aren't exactly sure what causes autism, they know that vaccines do not cause it. However, there are still misconceptions that connect vaccines to autism. This belief surged in 1998 after an article in a medical journal claimed that certain vaccines given to children were increasing the rate of autism. Not long after the paper was written, it was discovered that faulty research methods were used in the study. It was not credible.

Since then, many studies have been done to prove that vaccines do not cause ASD. In 2011, the Institute of Medicine (IOM) wrote a report on eight vaccines commonly given to children and found that all were safe. A follow-up study conducted by the Centers for Disease Control and Prevention (CDC) in 2013 looked at antigens. These are substances found in vaccines. They help the body make antibodies that fight diseases. The study found that children with autism and children without it had the same number of antigens from vaccines. This was evidence that vaccinations do not lead to autism.

Chapter
Four

Demographics

In 2000, the CDC launched the Autism and
Developmental Disabilities Monitoring (ADDM)
Network. The purpose of this network is to collect
information about how many children there are with
autism and other developmental disabilities living in
different regions of the United States. The ADDM's
2020 *Community Report on Autism* found that
1.85 percent of eight-year-old children had ASD, and
that the number of known children with this disorder
varied widely across the country. Colorado had the
lowest rate at 1.3 percent, while New Jersey had the
highest at 3.1 percent.[1]

Despite the data, the study notes, "Currently,
research does not show that living in certain
communities puts children at greater risk for
developing ASD." The study goes on to say that
the differences found across the country could be
due to how the ADDM Network finds children.

Boys are more likely to be diagnosed with
autism than girls. A person's biology may
play a role in this difference.

For instance, it may be able to only see children's health records in some areas, but in other states it may be able to identify children by both their special education and health records. The study said the difference "could also be due to changes in how children are identified and served in their local communities—for example, variations across communities in insurance coverage for ASD services." In addition, the study found that boys are four times more likely to be diagnosed with autism than girls.[2]

Race and Autism

Studies have also found differences when it comes to race and autism. In the past, the ADDM Network often found that more white children have been diagnosed with ASD than other races. But its 2020

White families typically have better access to health care compared with other races, which could be why white children with autism have been diagnosed more often.

report noted that, for the first time, there did not appear to be any difference in the rate of white and Black children diagnosed with autism by age eight.

However, the study did find that prevalence among white children still exceeded that among Hispanic children. Researchers believe the stigma of having a family member with a disability, a lack of health-care resources, and potentially not speaking English all contribute to underreporting by the Hispanic community. "These barriers mean that certain groups of children may not be getting the services they need to reach their full potential," the ADDM Network said.[4]

The study also reported that Black and Hispanic children with both ASD and an intellectual disability were diagnosed at later ages than white children who had both disorders. The CDC notes that *intellectual disability* is "a term used when there are limits to a person's ability to learn at an expected level and function in daily life."[5] The ADDM Network noted that the delay in diagnosis is a major issue since it "may limit opportunities [for children with autism] to receive services that could improve outcomes and quality of life."[6]

Often, autism research focuses on children. But it is a lifetime disorder, meaning it does not disappear with age. In the United States, half a million youth with autism will reach adulthood by 2025. A 2018 study added future births to this and found that the number of adults with autism could reach 2.8 percent of the population—almost three out of every 100 people.[8]

Global Statistics

Autism is not restricted by borders. It can be found in all countries and among all races and ethnicities. The World Health Organization (WHO) estimates one in 160 children has autism globally.[9] However, the WHO acknowledges that this is an average based on the data it has. The data does not represent information from low- and middle-income countries where the prevalence of autism is not known.

One of the biggest barriers to researching potential environmental causes for ASD is a lack of complete global data. Most countries do not track their population for ASD. For those countries that do have data, their criteria for diagnosing ASD vary, as do their data-collection methods.

Focus for Health is a foundation that looks at the role the environment plays in disorders, including autism. In 2017, Focus for Health went searching for the best ASD-prevalence data it could find from 17 countries. The range of prevalence was remarkable and highlights the problem with the differences in these diagnostic and data-collection methods. For instance, Hong Kong reported as many as one in 27 children having ASD, while Poland reported as few as one in 3,333.[12] There are several reasons for these discrepancies. Not all countries track and report autism rates. In other countries, the stigma of an autism diagnosis prevents parents from seeking help. And finally, there is not a global set of unified criteria on assessing and diagnosing autism. These factors skew the numbers.

Increase in Prevalence

The consistent increase in ASD cases over the years has not been explained and is worrisome to many people. There are theories as to why there has been an increase, but none fully provide an answer. There are

Hong Kong has the highest reported prevalence of autism in the world.

Older parents may be at a greater risk of having a child on the autism spectrum.

signs that older fathers and teenage or older mothers can increase the risk of ASD in children. And some research has shown that premature and underweight babies also have an increased risk.

However, most medical professionals believe the increase can be explained by more correct diagnoses. While there has been a consistent increase in the number of children diagnosed with ASD since 2000, a study from Penn State University found that two-thirds of that increase was matched by an equal decrease in diagnoses of children with intellectual disabilities.[14] Intellectual disabilities affect things such as learning, communicating, problem-solving, and the ability to take care of oneself. The research suggests that children with ASD were being misdiagnosed with intellectual or other developmental delays. That means there has not necessarily been an increase in autism cases.

"The majority of the increase [in autism prevalence] is due to progress in our ability to diagnose and identify people with autism in a broader spectrum than used to be possible."[15]

—Annette Estes, director of the University of Washington's Autism Center in Seattle

Chapter
Five

History and Research

ASD is a complicated disorder whose history is equally complex. Both its concept and definition have evolved greatly over the years. The earliest use of the term *autism* was by Swiss psychiatrist Eugen Bleuler in 1911. He used the term to group a set of features related to schizophrenia.

Today, people know that schizophrenia is a different disorder than ASD. Schizophrenia is a mental illness that can affect how a person feels, thinks, and behaves. People with this disease might not have a solid sense of reality. They can also experience delusions and hallucinations. Schizophrenic symptoms typically appear between the ages of 16 and 30 and aren't usually seen in children.

Medical professionals today know much more about ASD than when the disorder was first described in the early 1900s.

Bleuler outlined his definition of autistic thinking as a childlike desire to avoid unpleasant realities by replacing them with fantasies and hallucinations. Published in 1952, the *DSM-II* defined autism as a form of childhood schizophrenia marked by a detachment from reality. Up until the 1970s, a child displaying autistic symptoms would most likely have received a diagnosis of schizophrenia, which would be incorrect by today's standards.

The Early Researchers

Dr. Leo Kanner was a child psychiatrist at Johns Hopkins University School of Medicine. He was the first to use the term *autistic* to describe the features now commonly associated with the disorder. He wrote an influential paper in 1943 that described a group of children he had observed who all shared common mannerisms. These included being focused on or obsessed with objects, having little interest in socializing with others, and having a need for routine or resistance to unexpected change. Kanner also noted that these children had excellent rote memory, extreme sensory sensitivity, and a limited variety of spontaneous activity. He identified this as a new psychiatric disorder and called it infantile autism.

Dr. Leo Kanner was one of the first psychiatrists to study autism in detail.

Less than one year later, pediatrician Hans Asperger described children he had observed as having many of the same symptoms as Kanner's infantile autism. Both men believed that the social

Kanner or Asperger: Who Was First?

isolation they saw in their patients was an inborn trait that would carry on into adulthood. They also both observed a lack of eye contact and a resistance to change in the children. Finally, they noted that the children had limited or isolated interests in specific objects or topics. They also both differentiated the disorder from schizophrenia because the children showed these symptoms from very early childhood and did not have hallucinations.

However, the two doctors' reports did not align in all areas. The most distinct difference was in language skills. Kanner reported that a few of the children he observed did not speak at all, and the others did not use the vocabulary skills they had learned to communicate. By contrast, the children Asperger observed all had remarkable language skills for their age, using both freedom and originality in their language choices.

Another difference was in coordination. Kanner reported that most of his patients were clumsy in their gross motor skills but showed much more competence in their fine motor skills. On the other hand, Asperger reported his patients to be clumsy and awkward in both areas.

History of Institutionalization

Up until the 1970s, the most common advice given to parents of any children with special needs, including those with autism, was to institutionalize them. Upon examination, doctors would have explained to parents their child was "defective" and that the only course of action was to send the child away.[1] There was a lot of shame and stigma attached to having a special-needs child, so families tended not to talk openly about their situation and did not seek out advice or insight from other parents. Medical professionals considered keeping these children at home too much of a burden to the entire family, and so parents followed the advice of doctors even when they might not have wanted to. Between 1900 and 1923, the number of private facilities for people with disabilities grew. They were called farms, schools, institutes, hospitals, and academies. Most were overcrowded and residents often lacked quality care.

The final area where they found a difference was in learning. Kanner believed his patients learned best by rote memory. Asperger, on the other hand, thought his patients were abstract thinkers.

Diagnostic Shift

In the 1980s, psychiatrist Lorna Wing began to shift the diagnostic description of autism. She was the first researcher to view autism as a disorder on a spectrum that affected individuals of all intelligence levels and among all age groups, each in a unique way. Also, within her spectrum Wing developed a group of three subcategories to describe the different social approaches of children with autism: aloof children who were indifferent, passive children who accepted social interaction but did not seek it or actively engage in it, and active but unusual children who did seek social

Treating autism as a spectrum disorder allows people to get the types of interventions that are most helpful to them.

interaction but did so in an atypical way that usually resulted in rejection.

Wing also reviewed Asperger's findings, which had gone largely unnoticed. In 1981, she introduced his findings that centered around children with autism who acted like "little professors," according to Asperger.[3] These children were fascinated in only one or two subjects. They also had problems making friends, had repetitive behaviors, and were extremely uncomfortable with their routines being broken.

She coined the term *Asperger's syndrome* and used
it to further her research on autism as a spectrum
disorder. Wing also connected Kanner's research to
the spectrum.

On one end of the spectrum are people with
autism who are high functioning and have thriving
careers and lives. On the other end are people who
have more significant delays, such as those seen
in Kanner's research. They are withdrawn from
social groups, have sensory overloads, and display
obsessive, repetitive behaviors. In the middle of the
spectrum are people with autism who Wing noted
as having "a lack of ability to understand and use the
rules governing social behavior."[4]

In the mid-1990s, Wing was the first to suggest the
rate of prevalence was approximately 1 percent of the
population. Others believed that was exaggerated.
In 1996, she brought all her research and theories
together in her book *The Autistic Spectrum.* Over
time, many of her theories that were initially
challenged were proven to be correct.

Another key observation Wing made was that the
children in her study did not take part in imaginary
play. This observation led to another area of research
called theory of mind. Theory of mind is the ability

to understand the wants, beliefs, and intentions of others. This ability typically develops in children between the ages of three and five. Researcher Simon Baron-Cohen found that children with autism systematically failed a false-belief test while children of lower IQ passed it. A false-belief test checks whether an individual has the ability to understand that others may believe things that are not true. Baron-Cohen surmised that children with autism had a delay in development of theory of mind, which explained their lack of ability to interpret the actions and intentions of others.

—Uta Frith, professor of cognitive development at University College London

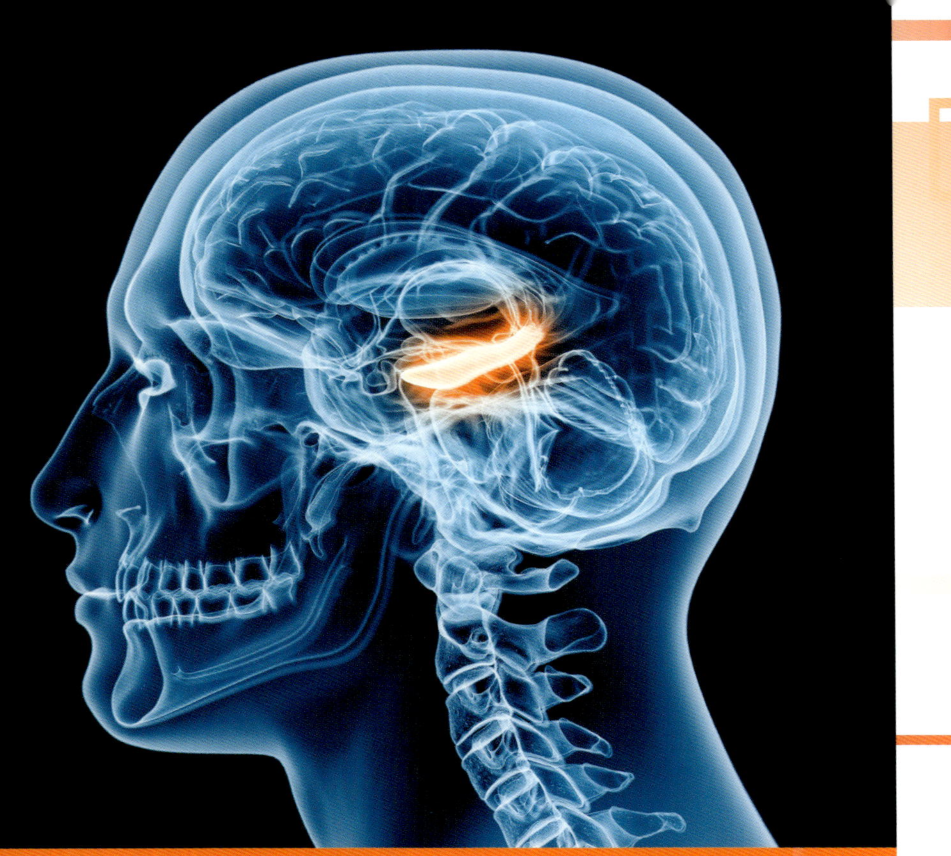

The hippocampus, *orange*, is the part of the brain that regulates emotion. Differences in hippocampal development may lead to ASD.

Biological Research

Dr. Margaret Bauman and Dr. Thomas Kemper have completed in-depth neurological research on potential causes of ASD. Their 1985 study found specific abnormalities in the brain cells of people with autism. Specifically, their research found that cells in the hippocampus, subiculum, and amygdala were smaller and more tightly packed together than in people who did not have autism.

The hippocampus regulates emotions, motivation, learning, and memory, while the amygdala plays a role in controlling emotion. The subiculum acts as a transmitter and receiver for the hippocampus. Bauman and Kemper's research suggested the abnormalities occurred at a cellular level and begin in early development. This opened the door to more biological research for the causes of ASD.

The *DSM*

Ongoing research has resulted in an evolving diagnostic description of autism. The *DSM-II* said

Eugenics

One concern some people with autism have is that genetic research will lead to eugenics. Eugenics is the pursuit of perfecting humanity through hereditary science. The fear is that if researchers found a gene that causes autism in a baby during pregnancy, that pregnancy would be ended. So, some people with autism think that the goal of researchers is not to help them, but rather prevent people with autism from being born in the first place. Alternatively, some people with autism fear that research might lead to genetic engineering that tries to normalize them. Since *abnormal* is not a descriptor with which some people with autism identify, *normal* is not a goal they are trying to achieve.

autism was a type of childhood schizophrenia. As more research continued and people learned more about the disorder, the definition had to change. The *DSM-III,* which was published in 1980, moved the description away from schizophrenia. Autism was listed as its own separate diagnosis and described as a pervasive developmental disorder (PDD).

This new diagnosis included three specific criteria: disinterest in people, impaired communication skills, and unusual responses to the environment—all appearing by 30 months of age. This was revised again in 1987 in the *DSM-III-R* to broaden the description to include milder symptoms and remove the age criteria. This update did not use the term *spectrum*, but it did include a list of 16 different criteria. Eight of these had to be met for a diagnosis of autism.

Published in 1994 and revised in 2000, the *DSM-IV* was the first edition of the manual to describe autism as a spectrum disorder. This version listed five disorders and reflected the beliefs that these conditions were of genetic origin and specific problems and interventions could be found for each. However, genetic research through the early 2000s found no genes that link exclusively to autism. Finding the root cause of these conditions was proving impossible, and therefore so too was finding specific interventions. The *DSM-5*, released in 2013, reflects this new understanding. For the first time, it defined all these conditions within a spectrum. It also created the new diagnostic category of ASD.

Chapter
Six

Early Intervention and Therapies

The therapy and intervention options available to help improve the lives of people with autism are as diverse as the disorder itself. Therapies and interventions that work well for some don't work as well for others. The Autism Society of America found that each family with a child who has autism has tried seven different therapies, on average.[1]

Most experts agree that early diagnosis and intervention are key to better functional outcomes for people with autism. The younger a child is diagnosed, the earlier health-care professionals can identify specific challenges and customize therapies and interventions. The interventions used depend

Some children with autism struggle with motor skills, such as holding on to or letting go of things. Early intervention can help them overcome these difficulties.

on the unique symptoms the patient has, but they can include applied behavior analysis (ABA), cognitive behavioral therapy (CBT), speech-language therapy, physical therapy, occupational therapy, pharmaceuticals, dietary and nutrition counseling, and participation in support groups.

Applied Behavior Analysis

ABA was first introduced as a method for treating autism in 1987 by Dr. Ivar Lovaas. He believed that social and behavioral skills could be taught to those with autism using ABA methods. Very simply, ABA is based on a command-and-reward system. It includes up to 40 hours of one-on-one therapy each week. Lessons can focus on many different skills, such as learning how to get dressed and brush one's teeth, how to write, or how to eat with a knife and fork.

The child is rewarded when specific steps are achieved and denied the reward when they are not. Many children who receive

"There are lots of different routes to adulthood. The profile we call autism might just be one of those routes."[2]

—Simon Baron-Cohen, professor of developmental psychopathology at the University of Cambridge intensive ABA training show an improvement in challenging behaviors. For this reason, it has become one of the most common forms of therapy for ASD. Some consider it one of the only scientifically valid therapies.

Other Therapeutic Interventions

CBT is a form of talk therapy used to help patients manage psychological issues through learning and practicing relaxation, coping, resilience, stress management, and assertiveness skills. When working with people who have autism, therapists are not treating ASD but rather the secondary conditions that their patients struggle with, such as anger, anxiety, aggression, depression, or difficulty with

Someone with autism may receive many types of therapies. Different therapies target different skills and aspects of daily living.

socialization. An example of this would be helping a person with autism recognize when he is feeling frustrated and about to get angry. A therapist might teach him to breathe and count to ten in an effort to control his temper.

A speech-language pathologist often plays a big role in a child's therapeutic plan. Speech problems can include only making sounds such as grunts and shrieks, talking in a singsong voice, or mumbling word-like sounds that do not have meaning.

Other communication problems can include lack of creative language and an inability to understand the meanings of words or symbols. Children with autism are facing not just the challenge of learning how to speak but also how to use language to communicate. A speech-language pathologist helps improve communication. For nonverbal patients, this might involve teaching sign language or using an electronic speaking device. For others, it might include doing facial exercises to improve articulation or speech. In all cases the goal is to improve communication and therefore relationships and quality of life for the person with autism.

Physical therapy would be recommended for those with comorbid physical disabilities, but it might also be suggested for people with autism to improve their gross motor coordination, build strength, and improve balance. The therapy is adapted to meet the individual abilities, needs, and goals of the patient. However, although physical therapy is a common intervention, there is no scientific evidence that any specific therapies improve movement skills in patients with autism.

Occupational therapists study human development and how people interact with their environments. An occupational therapist would be part of a therapeutic team to assess the social, emotional, and physical needs of the individual. The therapist works to develop a plan to help the individual achieve as much independence as possible at school, work, and home.

Pharmaceutical Interventions

There is no drug that treats or cures autism. Drugs are used either to treat symptoms of autism such as hyperactivity, attention deficit, impulsivity, anxiety, or depression, or to treat comorbid conditions such as digestion problems or seizures.

Some of these drugs, such as those for attention deficit or anxiety, might help settle patients so they are better able to absorb learning experiences. Addressing digestive problems might decrease physical discomfort and therefore improve behavior. There are also situations where antipsychotic medications have been used to address extreme behavior problems, but this is a controversial practice where children are concerned.

Nutrition Counseling

People with autism often have comorbid digestive or nutritional problems. Some common problems include reflux, diarrhea, allergies, and food sensitivities. Another common issue is a restricted

Some people with ASD are picky eaters. Sensory factors including the texture, color, temperature, and smell of the food can play a role in their eating habits.

diet due to a sensitivity to food textures. A lack of nutrients can compound already existing problems. A registered dietitian helps develop meal plans that ensure all nutritional requirements are met even when a restricted diet might be needed.

Some people believe that restricting certain foods can reduce autism symptoms. Two common restrictive diets are those that eliminate gluten, a protein found in wheat, and casein, a protein found in dairy. Trying these diets, however, is not recommended without medical consultation. There is no current evidence that supports these restrictive diets as ASD therapies, and in some cases limiting certain foods can do more harm than good.

Complementary and Alternative Medicines

Complementary and alternative medicines (CAMs) are all treatments and therapies that do not currently fall within the definition of traditional medicine. CAMs are popular among the autistic community. Approximately 28 percent of children with autism have received a CAM treatment, with one-third of them receiving one before they were diagnosed with ASD.[3] Biological CAM treatments include herbal or plant supplements and dietary interventions. Nonbiological CAM therapies include music, dance, or yoga therapy. They can also include massage, chiropractic, or acupuncture treatments.

A few biological CAM studies have produced some interesting results. For example, a 2012 study looked at the effect that probiotics, which are healthful yeasts and bacteria, would have on children with autism. Researchers gave children two probiotic capsules a day for two months. The authors reported improved symptoms of autism, including eye contact and proper recognition of facial expressions. However, this was a single study, and probiotics need to be researched and examined more.

Nonbiological CAMs have been studied a little more and show some promise. One 2012 study reported that children with autism who took part in yoga therapy showed a reduction in autistic behaviors. Researchers also found that muscle relaxation therapy gave children with autism more self-control, including control over their unruly behaviors. In addition, their parents reported a reduction in autistic symptoms. Participation in music therapy by both children and adults has shown improvements in social interactions and communication, with no negative side effects.

Even though there is a lack of scientific evidence to support the success of CAMs, these treatments are popular. Experts guess that this could be because people view them as natural and therefore safe. However, CAMs can be dangerous. Chelation, for example, is a treatment meant to remove mercury from the body. Proponents believe chelation therapy

Dogs Helping in Various Ways

There are three categories of dogs that can help people with autism. Companion dogs are most like regular pets. They give unconditional friendship, help teach important skills such as caring behaviors and responsibility, and encourage exercise. They are calm and well trained.

Therapy dogs are not certified but are more formally trained than companion dogs. They are a calming influence on people with autism. They can encourage social exchanges with others.

Service dogs are specially trained to meet the specific needs of the person they help. For example, they can calm an anxiety attack by leaning into the child or lying down on his or her lap. They can also interrupt self-injurious behavior with a gentle nudge. These dogs are certified and wear harnesses to show they are working. It is mandated that service dogs be allowed to enter all public areas, including restaurants.

Some studies have found that if parents participate in certain yoga therapies with their children who have autism, the children's behavior at home will improve.

cures ASD. However, there is no scientifically proven benefit, and the therapy can cause irreparable kidney damage.

Many CAMs are controversial, and there are questions surrounding the anecdotal evidence that supports them. Some are at best costly and at worst dangerous. Researchers are doing more studies to separate fact from fiction when it comes to these types of treatments.

Support Groups and Organizations

Support groups are perhaps one of the most beneficial therapies. Having good support not only helps an individual get what she needs to better cope with her disorder but also helps families learn how to manage the challenges of raising and living with a child on the autism spectrum. Support groups offer information, resources, and advocacy to people on the autism spectrum and their families. The benefits of joining a support group include finding people to vent frustrations and concerns to without judgment, feeling like you are no longer alone or isolated, sharing resources and strategies with others, accessing expert advice, and helping to fight depression.

National organizations such as the American Autism Association provide extensive resources to parents, including handbooks, workshops,

Support groups are a good way for families and individuals to connect over shared struggles with autism.

educational resources, and access to therapeutic recreation programs for low-income families. There are also social networks like MyAutismTeam where parents can find emotional support as well as advice and personal insight from other parents of children on the spectrum. Online forums provide opportunities for people on the spectrum to socialize without pressure or judgment. And in some cases, families form their own informal support groups in which they arrange social events and special activities for their communities. These people can come to feel like extended family and are valuable connections for all group members.

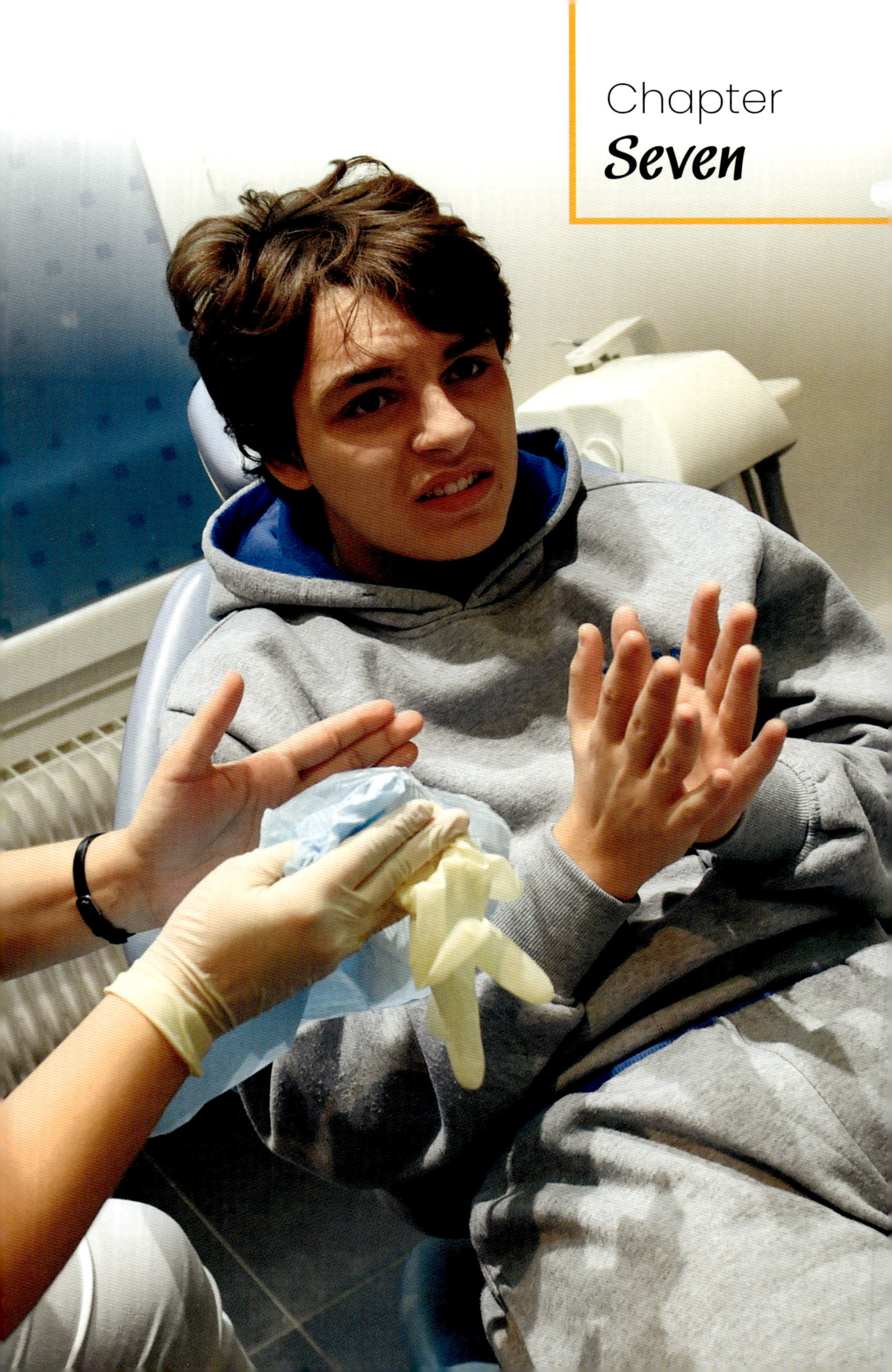
Chapter
Seven

Daily Life

The daily lives of people with autism are as diverse as those of neurotypical people. However, many things that neurotypical people take for granted, such as access to education, health care, therapies, employment, and social events, present barriers for people with autism. Everyday tasks and activities can feel overwhelming. Things such as going to school, attending a doctor appointment, working, or shopping might trigger sensory sensitivities that are stressful. Changes to routine or special events need to be communicated and planned for well in advance. Coping mechanisms can also be used to mitigate stress, such as wearing headphones to block loud noises or sunglasses inside to block bright lights. Shopping when stores are less busy is another strategy used to manage sensory overload.

It is not possible to define a typical day for a person on the autism spectrum because what is typical for one person might be quite unusual for another.

It can be difficult for someone with autism to stay calm and relaxed during nonroutine activities, such as dentist appointments.

Sensory-Friendly Spaces

People with autism need customized supports and therapies to help them get through their daily activities. For example, Matthew's days are not that much different than those of a typical 17-year-old boy—he does not need a lot of extra support in his day-to-day life. Some people on the autism spectrum have intellectual disabilities, extreme gross motor challenges, or self-injurious behaviors. Some do not communicate. Their days would look quite different from Matthew's. The degree of daily support and intervention varies from a few therapy sessions a week and a classroom aide to a full-time support worker who helps with all aspects of living, such as bathing and dressing.

Education

There are several different educational options available to children on the autism spectrum, including general classrooms both with and without supports, special-needs classrooms, or autism-only settings. Which choice is selected is dependent not only on individual needs but also on availability within school districts, as well as the financial resources of the parent. Regardless of which path is followed, by nature almost all educational settings are challenging for people on the autism spectrum. Quick verbal lessons, bright fluorescent lights, crowded spaces, and the inability to predict change all work together to create an incredibly stressful environment.

Many parents choose inclusion for their children. Inclusion places children in a typical classroom but provides them with extra supports and accommodations, such as a classroom aide and modified curriculum, so they have a better chance of success. Sadly, however, children with autism are often bullied and left out by other children in these traditional settings.

Children with autism might also be placed in special-needs classrooms. This can be a good environment because class sizes are generally small and the classroom can be more easily adapted to accommodate sensory sensitivity issues. Also, the children are usually included in regular school activities, such as joining other students in the cafeteria during mealtime. Generally, however, special-needs classes are designed for children who struggle academically. Unless the teacher is specially trained in working with children who have autism, these classrooms might not be ideal.

Some school districts provide smaller support classrooms. These classes have teachers and aides who are trained in how to handle children

Support classes can give children with autism the proper attention they need to develop important skills.

with autism. The classes also have a higher adult-to-student ratio than typical classrooms. They offer visual teaching and sometimes added interventions such as speech therapy or social skills exercises. The drawback to these classrooms is they can isolate children from the general school population. And sometimes a focus on social skills leads to neglect of academic teaching.

Employment and Financial Challenges

Each year, 50,000 youths with autism graduate high school in the United States, but more than one-third of them do not get a job or enroll in postsecondary education.[2] The changes to education, occupation, relationships, and routines that are part of becoming an adult can be stressful for people on the autism spectrum. After graduating, many young adults lose the support and services they got in high school and are sometimes left unsupported when they enter adulthood.

People on the autism spectrum have the lowest rate of employment among all disability groups. For those who are able and want to work, the process of seeking a job is challenging. Highly regarded job interview skills such as making eye contact, presenting with self-confidence, and having quick, articulate verbal responses are naturally a struggle for people with autism. Only 14 percent of people with autism who look for work end up working in a traditional paid setting.[3]

Teens with autism who do not pursue a college education tend to find more employment than those who have postsecondary education. The reason for this is because programs that offer employment counseling and job placement focus on low-skill jobs. There is a lack of support for those who have professional training and earn degrees. Often, parents and educators have low employment expectations for people with autism and therefore only look for and present limited options. More than half of adults on the spectrum work in a facility at unpaid activities with other people who have disabilities.[4]

For people with autism who do find jobs, there are more challenges to overcome on the work site. Anxiety, difficulty accepting criticism, resistance to change and working in groups, and sensory sensitivities all present barriers to successful integration into the workforce. Having to manage these stresses daily without accommodation from their employers often proves too difficult for some people, and they end up quitting their jobs.

Social Implications

As with every other aspect of ASD, the social implications of it vary widely. Most people on the autism spectrum have vastly different life experiences than neurotypical people. Children and youths with autism are necessarily dependent on their parents or caregivers for planning and managing their daily lives. Not much changes as they become adults. In addition to struggling to find employment, most adults with autism do not live independently. The 2017 National Autism Indicators Report found that 49 percent of adults with autism lived at home with their parents or another relative and 27 percent lived in a group home. Less than half were in complete control of their daily activities, such as deciding when to wake up and when to eat, and only 40 percent controlled their own finances.[5]

Meeting people, making friends, and taking part in social activities are all difficult for people on the autism spectrum. Although social awkwardness is a characteristic of autism, this does not mean that people with autism do not get lonely and do not want friends. The National Autism Indicators Report

Some people who have autism will always need outside support from family or friends.

found 41 percent of adults with autism felt lonely.[6] Fortunately, because of autism self-advocates and parents who get involved, there are online forums, children's camps, retreats for adults with autism, and many other events that provide social opportunities for the autism community while also catering to their needs and sensitivities.

Family

When one family member is diagnosed with autism, it affects all members of the family. Time, energy, and resources all tend to shift to focus on helping the person with autism. This can put a strain on marriages, relationships with other children, employment, and finances.

Having a child with autism compounds the stress of parenthood. Often, children with autism cannot communicate what they want or need. If parents cannot guess their child's need, it can cause the child to become frustrated. This, in turn, can lead to behavior problems that are sometimes aggressive and dangerous. It can also leave parents feeling frustrated and helpless. This is something that can play out repeatedly throughout the day. Parents can also find it difficult to explain and manage the behaviors of their child who has autism, so they might avoid public places such as restaurants or malls. They may even avoid visiting the homes of family

"One of the really positive outcomes of the fact that autism is becoming increasingly recognized is that people are seeing just how common it is, that at some level the stigma associated with having autism seems to be diminishing a little bit."[7]

—Dr. Bryan King, program director at the Autism Center at Seattle Children's Hospital and friends. This can lead to feelings of isolation for families.

Siblings of children with autism are also affected. The challenges they face can come from many places. Sometimes they are teased about their sibling, and this leaves them with feelings of embarrassment and then guilt for their embarrassment. Some feel that they need to make up for their sibling's autism by being perfect. Concern for their parents' well-being, as well as worry about their own future caregiving responsibilities, can also cause immense stress.

ASD has a negative financial impact on families too. Most intervention costs are not covered by government programs or insurance. Therefore, parents pay out of pocket for them. The expenses start early, with a first ASD assessment costing anywhere from $700 to $2,000.[8] ABA therapy can cost anywhere from $80 to $150 an hour, and a child might need ten to 40 hours a week.[9] Parents may also pay for additional services or treatments, such as speech pathology, equine therapy, and dietary supplements.

Strengths of Autism

People with ASD can face challenges, but some autism advocates note that the things that make people with autism different are in fact their strengths, not weaknesses. There are many famous and successful people with ASD, such as professor and activist Temple Grandin, comedic actor Dan Ackroyd, and filmmaker Tim Burton. People with autism can lead successful and independent lives, and some believe that autism contributed to their success rather than impeded it.

Some strengths of autism include an eye for detail and a focused approach to tasks. Many people with ASD also have an appreciation for simple pleasures, a direct and honest approach to communication, and

Organizations such as Spectrum Fusion work to bring adults with autism together and empower them.

a strong sense of right and wrong. Some are also very creative thinkers. All of these things provide people on the spectrum with a unique view of the world and an abstract approach to problem-solving. The neurodiversity movement is all about teaching society to see these differences as strengths and benefits, not weaknesses and drawbacks.

Chapter
Eight

Progress and Changes

As ASD assessments increase, so too does public awareness about people on the autism spectrum. With awareness, the stigma of ASD appears to be slowly decreasing. In addition, more diverse research studies are being conducted. Studies are looking into the biological causes of ASD, the prevalence of it, and effective autism interventions. Included in this is more research on adult autism to better understand lifelong needs and outcomes.

Artificial intelligence (AI) and robotics are areas of science that could change things dramatically. And the neurodiversity movement is shifting the conversation around autism. Rather than labeling it as a disorder, more people are recognizing those on the spectrum as different from typical but not damaged.

Major League Soccer teams helped raise autism awareness before a game in 2019.

Societal Changes

The increased rate of ASD prevalence over the past decade has brought ASD out of the shadows and into the spotlight. It is now more common for neurotypical people to know someone on the autism spectrum. Families are more open to talking about their relatives with autism. In addition, people with autism have gained a louder voice in their own discussion.

Although barriers to employment still exist, employers are slowly starting to understand the benefits of a neurodiverse workforce and are adapting both their hiring practices and work environments to accommodate more diverse workers. Auticon, for example, is an information technology company that has many staff members who are on the spectrum. Several generations of neurotypical people have now attended public schools or joined in recreational

"Who among us does not recognize the autistic scientist, whose clumsiness and lack of instincts have made him a familiar caricature, but who is capable of extraordinary accomplishments in a highly specialized field?"[1]

—Hans Asperger

activities alongside people with ASD, so they are more used to communicating and working with people who have this disorder. In addition, television shows such as *The Good Doctor*, *Atypical*, and *The A Word*, along with movies such as *Jack of Red Hearts* and *A Boy Called Po*, have all helped shine a light on and bring an element of normalcy to ASD.

Current and Future Research and Developments

Many people are conducting ASD research studies. For example, prenatal hormone levels and gut microbiomes in babies are two areas scientists are looking into as potential increased ASD risk factors. And nonpsychoactive cannabis is being researched for treating ASD symptoms. Genetic research continues as well. Google and the advocacy organization Autism Speaks have partnered to create MSSNG, a large autism genomic database. They plan to sequence the DNA of thousands of families affected by autism. This information will be made available to scientists around the globe to study and analyze through an open-source research platform. Their hope is that the information gathered will be used to personalize and improve treatments.

Adult autism is an area that needs more research. Little is known about the outcomes of adults living on the spectrum, and there are not many evidence-based programs for adults with ASD. According to a 2017 report from the US government's Interagency Autism Coordinating Committee, only 1 percent of all autism research funding goes to subjects related to adulthood.[2]

The age of AI is also introducing big changes to autism research and the lives of people with autism. AI applications are being developed to assist with assessment and diagnosis of ASD, as well as to help teach cognitive, social, and life skills. The US Food and Drug Administration approved a diagnosis tool developed by a company called Cognoa. Its program uses cutting-edge techniques such as machine learning, data mining, and predictive analytics, combined with parent-reported behavior, to give parents a personalized diagnosis and care options.

Empower Me is a product that teaches social skills using smart glasses. When wearing the glasses, a digital coach gives feedback to help the wearer gauge emotions and facial expressions in others. The coach might guide the wearer to make eye contact or monitor and comment on the wearer's anxiety and stress. Empower Me is meant to help people on the autism spectrum interact more effectively in the workplace.

Sometimes therapists struggle to work with children who have autism because the presence of the therapist causes sensory overload. QTrobot is a robot that is well-suited for these children. Lessons can be easier for the children when they are learning from a robot that does not display emotions. Therapists can personalize the lessons to the child's needs and abilities by programming the robot to follow specific instructions.

Neurodiversity Movement

The neurodiversity movement has led to some of
the biggest changes in both the direction of autism
research and how the autism community perceives
that research. Neurodiversity advocates do not like
ASD to be viewed as something that needs to be
cured, fixed, or eradicated. They view their autism
as something that makes them different from others,
but not damaged. They would like the direction
of ASD research to shift from cause and cure to
understanding, acceptance, and support.

Some studies are reporting results that support
the views of neurodiversity advocates. For example,
researchers found that some people with autism

were able to find their own solutions to overcoming barriers to the job market. They also found people with autism displayed talent in logical reasoning and visual perception, which are valuable assets that can be used in the workforce.

Companies such as Ford, Microsoft, and software company SAP have begun hiring more neurodiverse people. They note gains in productivity and a boost in innovation. These gains are explained by the very differences that neurodiverse people bring to an environment. They see and perceive things differently than neurotypical people do, so they identify problems and come up with solutions that neurotypical people may not think of.

There is a debate about whether autism should be viewed as a disability or an identity. People question whether researchers should continue to look for a cause and cure for autism. Others encourage people to see autism as a different way of being, advocating that researchers should look at ways to improve the lives of people with autism.

Essential *Facts*

Facts about Autism

- The *DSM-5* defines autism spectrum disorder (ASD) as a developmental disorder characterized by deficits in social communication and social interaction.

- One in 54 children in the United States has ASD. Males are four times more likely than females to be on the autism spectrum.

- The symptoms of ASD span a broad spectrum, and no two people with autism are the same.

- The cause of ASD is unknown. However, researchers believe it is mostly genetic with some environmental factors also at play.

- Vaccines do not cause ASD.

- There is not a single intervention or ASD therapy that is beneficial and effective for all people with autism.

- There is no cure for ASD.

How Autism Affects Daily Life

- Autism affects people in different ways. This is because people with autism are on a spectrum and each individual experiences different challenges.

- People with high-functioning autism are intelligent and may be fixated on one topic. They struggle with social skills.

- Some people with autism are low functioning and need help with day-to-day life. These individuals might struggle with nonverbal and verbal communication, have troubles in social situations, and have rigid routines and behaviors.

How Autism Can Be Managed

- Interventions and therapies are used to help people manage their autism. The earlier an individual is diagnosed with autism and is able to get intervention or therapy, the better his or her life outcomes could be.
- Some therapies and interventions include applied behavior analysis, cognitive behavioral therapy, speech-language therapy, physical therapy, and occupational therapy. Other interventions can include pharmaceuticals, dietary and nutrition counseling, and participation in support groups.
- Many people with autism do not want to be "cured." Instead, they see their differences as a benefit and embrace their individuality.

Quote

"Autism is a way of being. It is pervasive; it colors every experience, every sensation, perception, thought, emotion, and encounter, every aspect of existence. It is not possible to separate the autism from the person—and if it were possible, the person you'd have left would not be the same person you started with."

—Jim Sinclair, autism rights activist and individual on the spectrum

Glossary

antibody

A protein that the immune system uses to fight infection.

cognitive

Related to the act or process of thinking, reasoning, remembering, imagining, or learning.

correlation

A close match between factors.

diabetes

A disease in which a person's body doesn't properly process sugar.

DNA

Deoxyribonucleic acid, the chemical that is the basis of genetics, through which various traits are passed from parent to child.

fine motor skills

The movement of small muscles in a person's wrists and hands.

gene

A unit of hereditary information found in a chromosome.

gross motor skills

The movement of large muscles in a person's legs, arms, and torso.

intellectual disability

A disability characterized by significant deficits in learning ability.

neurodiversity

Defining atypical brain development as different, not damaged.

neuron

A cell that sends messages from the body to the brain and vice versa; a nerve cell.

neurotypical

Normal brain development.

prevalence

How widely present something is.

recurrence

A fresh instance of something that has already happened.

rote memory

The ability to recall information after it is repeated over and over.

spectrum

A broad range of features or symptoms.

stigma

A set of negative and often unfair beliefs that a society or group of people has about something.

viral

Related to or caused by a tiny parasite.

Additional Resources

Selected Bibliography

ADDM Network. "Community Report on Autism." *CDC*, 2020, cdc.gov. Accessed 22 June 2020.

"Autism Spectrum Disorder: Communication Problems in Children." *NIH*, Apr. 2020, nidcd.nih.gov. Accessed 7 Aug. 2020.

Evans, Bonnie. "How Autism Became Autism: The Radical Transformation of a Central Concept of Child Development in Britain." *History of the Human Sciences*, 2013, journals.sagepub.com. Accessed 22 June 2020.

Further Readings

Hand, Carol. *Handling ADHD*. Abdo, 2022.

Herschbach, Elisabeth. *What Is Autism?* ReferencePoint, 2021.

Hirschmann, Kris. *Kids and Autism*. ReferencePoint, 2019.

Online Resources

To learn more about handling autism, please visit **abdobooklinks.com** or scan this QR code. These links are routinely monitored and updated to provide the most current information available.

More Information

For more information on this subject, contact or visit the following organizations:

Autism Research Institute

833-281-7165
info@autism.org
autism.org
The Autism Research Institute conducts research to support the health and well-being of people with autism. It also advocates for the rights of these people and supplies resources to people on the spectrum, their families and health-care providers, and researchers.

Autism Society of America

6110 Executive Blvd., Ste. 305
Rockville, MD 20852
800-328-8476
autism-society.org
The Autism Society of America is a national organization with offices throughout the United States. Founded in 1965, it is a trusted source of information and resources about ASD.

Source Notes

CHAPTER 1. LIVING WITH AUTISM

1. "Autism in the Context of Ableism." *AUCD*, n.d., aucd.org. Accessed 21 Aug. 2020.

2. "Leading Perspectives on Disability: A Q&A with Dr. Stephen Shore." *Lime*, n.d., limeconnect.com. Accessed 21 Aug. 2020.

3. "Data & Statistics on Autism Spectrum Disorder." *CDC*, 25 Mar. 2020, cdc.gov. Accessed 21 Aug. 2020.

CHAPTER 2. SYMPTOMS AND DIAGNOSIS

1. Katharine Zuckerman et al. "Timeliness of Autism Spectrum Disorder Diagnosis and Use of Services among US Elementary School-Aged Children." *Psychiatric Services*, 1 Aug. 2016, ps.psychiatryonline.org. Accessed 21 Aug. 2020.

2. Barnbaum, Deborah R. *The Ethics of Autism*. Indiana UP, 2008. 137.

3. "Girls on the Autism Spectrum Are Being Overlooked." *Duke University School of Medicine*, 28 Mar. 2018, ipmh.duke.edu. Accessed 21 Aug. 2020.

4. Shubhrajan Wadyal. "Why Autism in Girls Is Often Missed until Adulthood." *AMITA Health*, n.d., amitahealth.org. Accessed 21 Aug. 2020.

5. "Autism's Clinical Companions: Frequent Comorbidities with ASD." *Children's Hospital of Philadelphia*, 1 July 2017, chop.edu. Accessed 21 Aug. 2020.

6. "Fragile X Syndrome." *Spectrum News*, n.d., spectrumnews.org. Accessed 21 Aug. 2020.

CHAPTER 3. CAUSES OF AUTISM

1. Matt Warren. "Autistic Children May Inherit DNA Mutations from Their Fathers." *Science*, 19 Apr. 2018, sciencemag.org. Accessed 21 Aug. 2020.

2. Nicholette Zeliadt. "Autism Genetics, Explained." *Spectrum News*, 27 June 2017, spectrumnews.org. Accessed 21 Aug. 2020.

3. "Mental Disorders and Disabilities among Low-Income Children." *NCBI*, 2015, ncbi.nlm.nih.gov. Accessed 23 Sept. 2020.

4. Knvul Sheikh. "In Autistic Children, Low Intelligence Forecasts Later Difficulties." *Spectrum News*, 25 Mar. 2019, spectrumnews.org. Accessed 21 Aug. 2020.

5. Zeliadt, "Autism Genetics, Explained."

6. Neil Risch et al. "Familial Recurrence of Autism Spectrum Disorder: Evaluating Genetic and Environmental Contributions." *American Journal of Psychiatry*, Nov. 2014, pubmed.ncbi.nlm.nih.gov. Accessed 21 Aug. 2020.

7. E. J. Mundell. "Autism Largely Caused by Genetics, Not Environment." *WebMD*, 17 July 2019, webmd.com. Accessed 21 Aug. 2020.

8. Zeliadt, "Autism Genetics, Explained."

9. "SHANK3." *Spectrum News*, n.d., spectrumnews.org. Accessed 21 Aug. 2020.

10. Mundell, "Autism Largely Caused by Genetics."

11. "What Is Phelan-McDermid Syndrome?" *PMSF*, n.d., pmsf.org. Accessed 21 Aug. 2020.

12. Brian Lee. "Autism Heritability: It Probably Does Not Mean What You Think It Means." *Spectrum News*, 7 Jan. 2020, spectrumnews.org. Accessed 21 Aug. 2020.

13. Erin Blakemore. "Psychologists Once Blamed 'Refrigerator Moms' for Their Kids' Autism." *History*, 22 Aug. 2018, history.com. Accessed 21 Aug. 2020.

14. Kristen Lyall et al. "The Changing Epidemiology of Autism Spectrum Disorders." *Annual Review of Public Health*, 14 June 2019, ncbi.nlm.nih.gov. Accessed 21 Aug. 2020.

CHAPTER 4. DEMOGRAPHICS

1. "Community Report on Autism." *CDC*, 2020, cdc.gov. Accessed 21 Aug. 2020.

2. "Community Report on Autism."

3. "Autism Rate Rises 43 Percent in New Jersey, Study Finds." *Science Daily*, 11 Apr. 2019, sciencedaily.com. Accessed 21 Aug. 2020.

4. "Community Report on Autism."

5. "Facts about Intellectual Disability." *CDC*, 25 Oct. 2019, cdc.gov. Accessed 21 Aug. 2020.

6. "Community Report on Autism."

7. "Community Report on Autism."

8. Diana E. Schendel and Erla Thorsteinsson. "Cumulative Incidence of Autism into Adulthood for Birth Cohorts in

Denmark, 1980–2012." *JAMA Network*, 2018, jamanetwork.com. Accessed 21 Aug. 2020.

9. "Autism Spectrum Disorders." *World Health Organization*, 7 Nov. 2019, who.int. Accessed 21 Aug. 2020.

10. Ariane V. S. Buescher et al. "Costs of Autism Spectrum Disorders in the United Kingdom and the United States." *NIH*, Aug. 2014, pubmed.ncbi.nlm.nih.gov. Accessed 21 Aug. 2020.

11. J. Paul Leigh and Juan Du. "Brief Report: Forecasting the Economic Burden of Autism in 2015 and 2025 in the United States." *NIH*, Dec. 2015, pubmed.ncbi.nlm.nih.gov. Accessed 21 Aug. 2020.

12. Robyn Charron. "Autism Rates across the Developed World." *Focus for Health*, 28 Aug. 2017, focusforhealth.org. Accessed 21 Aug. 2020.

13. Charron, "Autism Rates across the Developed World."

14. Warren Cornwall. "Autism Rates Are Up, but Is It Really on the Rise?" *Science*, 22 July 2015, sciencemag.org. Accessed 21 Aug. 2020.

15. Cornwall, "Autism Rates Are Up, but Is It Really on the Rise?"

CHAPTER 5. HISTORY AND RESEARCH

1. John Donvan and Caren Zucker. *In a Different Key: The Story of Autism*. Crown, 2016. 24.

2. Rachel Nuwer. "A Brief History of Autism Research." *Atlantic*, 15 Mar. 2016, theatlantic.com. Accessed 21 Aug. 2020.

3. Paul Vitello. "Dr. Lorna Wing, Who Broadened Views of Autism, Dies at 85." *New York Times*, 19 June 2014, nytimes.com. Accessed 21 Aug. 2020.

4. Vitello, "Dr. Lorna Wing Dies at 85."

5. Francesca Happé and Simon Baron-Cohen. "Remembering Lorna Wing." *Spectrum News*, 15 July 2014, spectrumnews.org. Accessed 21 Aug. 2020.

CHAPTER 6. EARLY INTERVENTION AND THERAPIES

1. Natascia Brondino. "Complementary and Alternative Therapies for Autism Spectrum Disorder." *Hindawi*, 2015, hindawi.com. Accessed 21 Aug. 2020.

2. Moheb Costandi. "Simon Baron-Cohen: Theorizing on the Mind in Autism." *Spectrum News*, 9 May 2011, spectrumnews.org. Accessed 21 Aug. 2020.

3. Brondino, "Complementary and Alternative Therapies for Autism Spectrum Disorder."

4. Maureen O'Toole. Personal interview. 16 Mar. 2020.

CHAPTER 7. DAILY LIFE

1. Nicolas Bommarito. *Inner Virtue*. Oxford UP, 2018. 111.

2. "National Autism Indicators Report." *Autism Institute*, 2017, drexel.edu. Accessed 21 Aug. 2020.

3. Anne M. Roux et al. "National Autism Indicators Report: Developmental Disability Services and Outcomes in Adulthood." *Drexel University*, 24 May 2017, drexel.edu. Accessed 21 Aug. 2020.

4. Roux et al., "National Autism Indicators Report."

5. Roux et al., "National Autism Indicators Report."

6. Roux et al., "National Autism Indicators Report."

7. Kari Vandraiss. "A Day in a Life with Autism." *425 Magazine*, 31 May 2013, 425magazine.com. Accessed 21 Aug. 2020.

8. "The Cost of Autism Diagnostic Testing Can Be Quite Expensive." *Clarifi*, n.d., clarifiasd.com. Accessed 21 Aug. 2020.

9. "The Cost of Raising a Child with Autism." *Polk County DAC*, 1 Aug. 2018, polkcountydac.com. Accessed 21 Aug. 2020.

CHAPTER 8. PROGRESS AND CHANGES

1. Steve Silberman. *NeuroTribes*. Penguin, 2015. 139.

2. Anne M. Roux et al. "National Autism Indicators Report: Developmental Disability Services and Outcomes in Adulthood." *Drexel University*, 24 May 2017, drexel.edu. Accessed 21 Aug. 2020.

3. "Secretary-General's Message on World Autism Awareness Day." *United Nations*, 2 Apr. 2014, un.org. Accessed 21 Aug. 2020.

Index

About the Author

Racquel Foran

Racquel Foran is a freelance writer from Coquitlam, British Columbia, Canada. She has authored several nonfiction titles for school-age readers covering diverse subjects such as organ transplants, robotics, and North Korea, among others. When she is not writing, Foran enjoys tending to her little free library, painting, and walking her dogs by the river.

About the Consultant

Cassandra Sanchez, PsyD

Cassandra Sanchez, PsyD, is a clinical psychology postdoctoral fellow at the University of Southern California's University Center for Excellence in Developmental Disabilities. Her clinical expertise is in psychodiagnostic assessment, particularly in the differential diagnosis of ASD, with children ages birth to five. Dr. Sanchez lives in sunny Los Angeles, California, where she enjoys reading on the beach and occasionally escaping to her hometown in the San Francisco Bay Area.